Little Pebble™

Our Pets

Cats

by Lisa J. Amstutz

CAPSTONE PRESS
a capstone imprint

Little Pebble is published by Capstone Press,
1710 Roe Crest Drive, North Mankato, Minnesota 56003
www.mycapstone.com

Library of Congress Cataloging-in-Publication Data
Names: Amstutz, Lisa J., author.
Title: Cats / by Lisa Amstutz.
Description: North Mankato, Minnesota : an imprint of Capstone Press, [2018]
    | Series: Our pets | Audience: Age 4–8. | Audience: K to Grade 3. |
    Description based on print version record and CIP data provided by
    publisher; resource not viewed.
Identifiers: LCCN 2017028019 (print) | LCCN 2017029628 (ebook) |
    ISBN 9781543501797 (eBook PDF) | ISBN 9781543501605 (hardcover) |
    ISBN 9781543501674 (paperback)
Subjects: LCSH: Cats—Juvenile literature.
Classification: LCC SF445.7 (ebook) | LCC SF445.7 .A47 2018 (print) | DDC
    636.8—dc23
LC record available at https://lccn.loc.gov/2017028019

Editorial Credits
Marissa Kirkman, editor; Juliette Peters (cover) and Charmaine Whitman (interior), designers;
Morgan Walters, media researcher; Laura Manthe, production specialist

Image Credits
Getty Images: KidStock, 5; Shutterstock: 5 second Studio, top 7, Africa Studio, bottom 21,
ANURAK PONGPATIMET, top 21, Bogdan Sonjachnyj, left 9, Borja Laria, right 9, fantom_rd,
15, Grey Carnation, 17, ILonika, bottom 7, ka pong26, 11, Kalmatsuy, back cover, MaraZe,
19, MNStudio, Cover, Mr Aesthetics, (wood) design element throughout, Okssi, left 13, Seika
Chujo, 1, Yimmyphotography, top 13

Printed and bound in the United States of America.
010881S18

Table of Contents

Listen! 4

All About Cats 8

Growing Up 16

Playful Pets 20

Glossary 22
Read More 23
Internet Sites 23
Critical Thinking Questions . 24
Index 24

Listen!

Meow!

A cat rubs your leg.

It wants to be petted.

Cats make other sounds too.

Happy cats purr.

Angry cats hiss.

All About Cats

Some cats have long hair.

Other cats have short hair.

Cats lick their hair

to keep it clean.

Some cats are one color.

Calico cats have patches.

Their hair is orange,

white, and black.

Tabby cats have stripes.

calico

tabby

Cats have claws on their toes.

They scratch often.

This keeps their claws sharp.

claws

Cats have some very

good senses.

They see well in the dark.

Cats can hear well too.

They feel with their whiskers.

Growing Up

Look!

It is a litter of kittens.

They drink milk

from their mother.

After four weeks,
kittens eat cat food.
Yum!

Playful Pets

Cats like to play with you.

They chase toys.

This cat hides in a box.

Peek!

Glossary

angry—a feeling of being upset and unhappy

claw—a hard curved nail on the foot of an animal

hiss—to make a "sss" sound like a snake

kitten—a young cat

litter—a group of animals born at the same time to one mother

meow—the noise a cat makes

purr—to make a low, soft sound

sense—a way of knowing about your surroundings; hearing, smelling, touching, tasting, and sight are senses

whisker—a long stiff hair growing on the face and bodies of some animals

Read More

Gardeski, Christina Mia. *Cats: Questions and Answers.* Pet Questions and Answers. North Mankato, Minn.: Capstone Press, 2017.

Graubart, Norman. *My Cat.* Pets are Awesome! New York: PowerKids Press, 2014.

Murray, Julie. *Cats.* Family Pets. Minneapolis: ABDO Kids, 2016.

Internet Sites

Use FactHound to find Internet sites related to this book.

Visit www.facthound.com

Just type in 9781543501605 and go.

Check out projects, games and lots more at
www.capstonekids.com

Critical Thinking Questions

1. Would you like to own a cat? Why or why not?

2. Why is it important for cats to scratch?

3. What does a calico cat look like?

Index

calicos, 10

claws, 12

food, 18

hair, 8, 10

kittens, 16, 18

senses, 14

sounds, 6

tabbies, 10

whiskers, 14